Five-Senses Journal

Access the Present Moment and Rediscover Your Wonder and Curiosity

CLAUDIUS

ISBN: 978-1-6847-0059-2 (sc)
ISBN: 978-1-6847-0066-0 (e)

Lulu Publishing Services rev. date: 04/22/2019

This project is dedicated to You! The inspiration, courage, and Love you have shown are some of the greatest gifts I will ever receive. With all my heart, thank you.

Acknowledgments

First, I would like to say thank you to the owner of this journal. You are a person who wants to learn, grow, and expand. Your desire to understand who you are and take responsibility for that immense undertaking is inspiring. Continue to be a light in this world where the diffusion of responsibility is so common. Show the benefits of being the wonderful individual you are.

Mom, I miss you every day. Thank you for teaching me the importance of finding peace. I love you.

Dad, your persistence and grit keep me moving forward. I am honored to have you as my father and showing me the importance of following a dream to the end. I love you.

Brother, I really look up to you. Though I am physically taller (ha ha!), the way you hold yourself in this world and how you treat your family and others will always have me looking up to you. I love you.

The tribe. You guys and gals are the reason I am here. Your insatiable appetite for learning has brought me to this point. In trying to keep up, I have become a version of myself I dreamt of as a child. You were there for me during thick and thin. I can't thank you enough. We will reunite one day. I love you all.

Finally, to those teachers out there who make their lives so public and known: Tim Ferriss, Dave Asprey, Tony Robbins, Joe Rogan, and Dan Carlin—the list could go on forever. Thank you for being willing to be in the public eye and for making the world a better place.

Life is weird but in a cool way.
—Anonymous

The world is a weird and wonderful place. From the smells of fresh-baked pastries in the morning to the touch of a loved one's hand, the experiences we can have are immeasurable and unique. Yet how often do we move past them without even noticing what just happened? How often are we so wrapped up in our thoughts of other places or times that we miss the magic happening right before us? Each day, each minute, each moment is its very own collection of events and occurrences that will only happen then and there. If we can learn to take in the moment and sense the seemingly old or mundane with renewed curiosity, the world will transform from a never-ending slog of repetitive days and events to a vibrant experience that we can have whenever we choose.

I created the *Five-Senses Journal* to give you the skills and tool kit to return to the moment and see the wonder in life again. Our brains are designed to process stimuli so that we can move through the world with ease—without having to consciously decide where to put our attention. This is an amazing adaptation; it allows us to move through the world efficiently. We don't have to choose where to put our attention and what to ignore. It helps us navigate a busy day with ease and comfort. The problem arises when we do not know how to shut it off. We allow the wonders of life to slip on by because our brains are familiar with them. *Oh, that's a tree. Just keep walking. I know what a tree is,* the brain says. *My wife—well, I have known her for ten years. There is nothing more to her that I don't already know,* we may assume. *That is cool. The snow is falling, but I have seen that before.*

We move on to the next task. This is the brain labeling what we assume we know in order to conserve energy. The reality is that each person, object, experience, or moment is so vast and expansive that, with the right tools, we could be curious forever. So, what if you could choose to allow the novelty that we normally skip over to enter into the forefront of your focus? What if you could see a tree with a renewed sense of captivating wonder, learn the smallest details about your partner, experiencing details that make the person's infinite being shine forth, or see snowfall through the eyes of a child again? What if you could move into a space of stillness and inner peace where you'd become fully connected to the world around you? It can remove boredom, stagnation, and monotony while bringing you into an experience of wonder, excitement, and connectedness that enhances the overall quality of your life. Through your five senses, this reality is possible.

The benefits of this practice can be seen across a wide variety of aspects in your life. Bringing your attention into the present moment can increase mindfulness, motivation, focus, and centeredness. All of which will be discussed in further detail. If you are curious, the scientific research supporting the claims can be found using the references.

What You Will Gain

Mindfulness

Mindfulness is the ability to be present in the here and now. We are mindful when we observe events around us without judgments or criticisms. This is a skill that can be learned, just like learning to cook a favorite meal. Mindfulness has been a human skill for more than five thousand years, and scientists are now studying its benefits. In a systematic review (a study of multiple studies) done in 2006, researchers found that mindfulness through meditation improved anxiety and mood.[1] Additionally, researchers found improvements in symptoms of pain and depression and also improved quality of life.[2] Mindfulness is a powerful tool that we can learn by using our own five senses.

Motivation

Some of these details may feel repetitive, but it is by design. Learning and understanding takes time and repetition. I want you to have a clear grasp on the benefits to help with the motivation to continue the *Five-Senses Journal*. The human brain is a wonderful pattern-making machine. It can create patterns out of chaotic environments to help determine the best course of action. The brain takes in all the information around us, processes it, and spits out the most efficient behaviors to engage in. Remember, this is not a bad thing! However, we can also gloss over some

---

[1]   Arias, A. J., Steinberg, K., Banga, A., & Trestman, R. L. (2006). "Systematic Review of the Efficacy of Meditation Techniques as Treatments for Medical Illness." *The Journal of Alternative and Complementary Medicine,* 12 (8).

[2]   Ibid.

incredible things. The brain loves to categorize as part of its efficiency model, so it tells us a tree is a tree just like the last twenty-five trees we walked past today. But as a result of this pattern-making process, we can miss the beautiful and novel details of each and every tree. It is not just trees but everything you can imagine. This is important because novelty is associated with release of dopamine and oxytocin, which have been found to increase motivation.[3] By learning to see novelty in the everyday experience, you will also stimulate the release of dopamine and oxytocin, creating more motivation through your day. Free motivation anytime you like? Sounds like a pretty sweet deal.

Focus

In the current world, something always seems to be vying for our attention. A text message, a Facebook notification, or in my case, the World Cup playing in the background as I write this can pull our attention away from our tasks or this moment. Practicing focusing on the details of an object can strengthen directed attention, just as we develop our muscles through practice. *Time* magazine published an article discussing meditation and its benefits for focus. The article stated that there is an increase in focus after only three months of five hours of meditation a day! No need to fret—there were also benefits in focus from using mindfulness only five minutes a day.[4] Let your five senses be a gateway into a world of focus and attention whenever you choose.

[3]   Machelska, H. (2016). "Faculty of 1,000 evaluation for Mindfulness Meditation for Chronic Pain: Systematic Review and Meta-analysis." *F1000—Postpublication Peer Review of the Biomedical Literature.*

[4]   Cell Press. (2006, August 27). "Pure Novelty Spurs the Brain." *ScienceDaily.* Retrieved June 26, 2018 from www.sciencedaily.com/releases/2006/08/060826180547.htm

Centeredness

With all the demands in life today, it is hard to feel connected to your inner self, which we feel when we are in line with our beliefs, attitudes, and actions. It is the self we feel at home with. Many times, we are pulled in many directions to please our bosses, friends, and even family. It can be difficult to find who we truly are at the depths of our core.

As you learn to notice details in the outside world, your focus will shift to the inner world. Bringing attention to feelings of the inner world can help you understand the subtle differences within you and how to truly align yourself. You might begin to experience feelings of joy or satisfaction while writing a work proposal or during a hard workout. These can be subtle shifts in your experience, which could be easily glossed over.

By being aware of the shifts, you can identify the things that truly make you feel engaged in your life. Do these activities more, feel engaged more, and experience a truly centered you. One study showed that meditation allows people to more quickly attend to their subconscious impulses on command.[5] This would indicate a better awareness to the changes that occur in your emotional experiences, which could lead to you doing more of the things that make you happy.

Using this meditation and feeling those experiences fully can allow you to create your reality. Through the five senses, you can bring your awareness inside to truly know yourself. Allow this practice to be your form of mindfulness meditation. Reap the benefits that meditation provides through your five senses.

---

[5]   "Losing Focus? Studies Say Meditations May Help." http://content.time.com/time/health/article/0,8599,2008914,00.html

How to Use the Journal

The *Five-Senses Journal* is broken up into three sections, each lasting thirty days. The first is notice: taking in the outside world. The second is observe: placing your awareness on your internal states. Finally, stillness, which moves your experience into silence without words. More to come on each section later.

After the ninety days, you will be able to slow down and experience all the wonder each moment can offer. The journal should be used every day. Through your own senses, you will notice minute details about the world around you as well as yourself. The activities for each sense can be practiced back-to-back or separately throughout the day; it is up to you. Initially, do the practices in an area where you can isolate a particular sense (it's impossible to do this completely, but a quiet, tranquil area can be beneficial to start).

During the activities, you will choose one sense to focus on and one stimulus to attend to. For example, if you are working with sight, you can choose a flower and look at it with curiosity and focus for one to two minutes. Once you are done, you can write down your observations in your journal. Do this for each sense every day. You can choose any stimulus you want, with certain days containing recommendations for a certain type of stimuli (a person, something you don't particularly like, etc.).

Each month you participate in the journal, the focus of your attention will change. It will shift from the external to the internal and from words to feelings and connection. You will move through *noticing* the external object to *observing* your inner state in relation to the object and finally to *stillness* in which you fully connect with the object and yourself beyond words.

Each page provides a place to write your observations as your vocabulary and eye for detail grow. There are two lists of words in the appendix that can help describe observations during your practice. There is a specific area to reflect on your experience in the evening. These reflections can describe the difference in mood you may have felt, how your day changed after doing your practice, or how you want to try something new for the next day. It is important to recapture those feelings and experiences each night to help the brain recognize your goals and objectives. I provide specific examples before each month of journaling.

Aldous Huxley describes the mission of this journal in *The Divine Within,* a collection of essays. The mission statement is pulled from the essay "Who Are We?"

> We have to combine these things: to walk on this tightrope, to gather the data of perception, to be able to analyze it in terms of language, at the same time to be able to drop the language and to go on into the experience. It is very, very delicate and difficult.[6]

Let us begin to walk this tightrope between language and experience. To experience life the way you have always wanted, find the life that is most fulfilling to you.

---

6   Huxley, Aldous, and Huston Smith. *The Divine Within: Selected Writings on Enlightenment.* Harper Perennial, 2013.

PART I

Notice

The first step is to learn how to notice differences in your environment. Instead of glossing over a scene you have seemingly seen thousands of times, you will learn to appreciate subtle details in the same scene. You will choose items, sounds, food, people, and whatever else you encounter and practice sensing new details you have never noticed before. Really sense a stimulus you think you know well with renewed curiosity; don't pull from past experiences but from the direct interaction in that moment. Take your time as you experience the item. Spend one to two minutes sensing all the newness it has to offer. Close your eyes, take it in, and then notice it again with even more curiosity. As you notice, write all the details you sense—as many or as few as you like. The goal is to understand that every moment is unique and every experience is different from the last. You will cultivate a new skill set of noticing and appreciating subtle details.

Example

Never say there is nothing beautiful in the world
anymore. There is always something to make you wonder
in the shape of a tree, the trembling of a leaf.
—Albert Schweitzer

Sight: _____ Lime _____

Green with yellow running through. Small dimple-like shapes beneath a clear layer of skin. Small brown dots scattered throughout. Small vein-looking remains in a circular shape where the lime connected to the tree.

Smell: _____ Cooked Rice _____

Sweet and nutty smell. It reminds me of the Cream of Wheat breakfast I would have as a child. Slight burnt smell.

Touch: _____ Avocado _____

The top is narrower than the bottom. The skin of the avocado is smooth, and there are some rough spots, bumps, and imperfections. The top is rough and dry. It felt firm when I squeezed it, but it also gave way to my grip a bit.

Taste: _____ Coffee _____

The initial flavor had a slight tanginess with hints of earthy flavors. A subtle sweetness underlies it all. Then, as the coffee sits on the tongue, there is a slight bitterness.

Hearing: _____Water in the Sink_____

There was the sound of the water being pressed through the faucet. It sounded like a low-pitched hiss, which I will call *flisk*. Then the water moved into the sink, creating a swishing, swooshing sound.

Evening Reflection:

It was difficult to describe certain senses, hearing and smell particularly. While I was focused on noticing the items, I felt calm and relaxed. There was a feeling of harmony in my thoughts without the insistent chatter that typically occurs. I also wonder if those veins I described on the lime are used for that function. I am going to look it up.

> Look up at the stars and not down at your feet. Try
> to make sense of what you see and wonder about
> what makes the universe exist. Be curious.
> —Stephen Hawking

Sight: __My Desk__

space exists here, grandpa looks at me, my oba, auntie, books and journal. metallic surface reflects it back to me, wooden animals, Carol's US flag flutters in the wind outside

Smell: __The smell of fritos and cheese, one of my favorite__

smell. earthy, grounding smells. well-rounded, not sour or sweet but savory and yummy. the smell of multiple people on the couch but above all, the smell of my lovely Coco ♥

Touch: __Sun's warmth on my back. Heat increasing there__

warmth travels up to shoulders. Tingling sensation when I shift. I raise my shirt, feel tingling heat directly on my skin, penetrating into my skin, cooking it

Taste: __Toothpaste__

Baking soda and natural oils fill my lower tongue, on each side. It has an alkaline taste, not strong but there, neutralizing all other tastes in my mouth & breath

Hearing: __Silence & Buzzing Sound in my room__

sounds like an electric buzz, in both ears. electric crickets the wind courses outside, it increases in depth. a car streaks down the road. And another. my hand brushes against paper. a whipping sound.

Evening Reflection:

How wonderful that...
I am beginning to use my 5 senses more
I was able to meditate between bootcamp sessions
I'm getting $4,000 back in taxes! ★

To be more childlike, you don't have to give up being an adult.
The fully integrated person is capable of being both an adult
and a child simultaneously. Recapture the childlike feelings of
wide-eyed excitement, spontaneous appreciation, cutting loose,
and being full of awe and wonder at this magnificent universe.
—Wayne Dyer

Sight: _____

_____

_____

_____

Smell: _____

_____

_____

_____

Touch: _____

_____

_____

_____

Taste: _____

_____

_____

_____

Hearing: _____

_____

_____

_____

Evening Reflection:

_____

_____

_____

_____

Passion isn't something that lives way up in the sky, in abstract dreams and hopes. It lives at ground level, in the specific details of what you're actually doing every day.
—Marcus Buckingham

Sight: _____

_____

_____

_____

Smell: _____

_____

_____

_____

Touch: _____

_____

_____

_____

Taste: _____

_____

_____

_____

Hearing: _____

_____

_____

_____

Evening Reflection:

_____

_____

_____

_____

Recommendation: Use a person once this week during your practice. For example: you can hold someone's hand and feel their skin against yours, look deeply into their eyes, or taste their lips.

Sight: _____

_____

_____

_____

Smell: _____

_____

_____

_____

Touch: _____

_____

_____

_____

Taste: _____

_____

_____

_____

Hearing: _____

_____

_____

_____

Evening Reflection:

_____

_____

_____

_____

Wisdom begins in wonder.
—Socrates

Sight: _____

_____
_____
_____

Smell: _____

_____
_____
_____

Touch: _____

_____
_____
_____

Taste: _____

_____
_____
_____

Hearing: _____

_____
_____
_____

Evening Reflection:

_____
_____
_____
_____

He who marvels at the beauty of the world in summer will
find equal cause for wonder and admiration in winter.
—John Burroughs

Sight: _____

_____
_____
_____

Smell: _____

_____
_____
_____

Touch: _____

_____
_____
_____

Taste: _____

_____
_____
_____

Hearing: _____

_____
_____
_____

Evening Reflection:

_____
_____
_____
_____

Cherish sunsets, wild creatures, and wild places. Have a
love affair with the wonder and beauty of the earth.
—Stewart Udall

Sight: _____

_____
_____
_____

Smell: _____

_____
_____
_____

Touch: _____

_____
_____
_____

Taste: _____

_____
_____
_____

Hearing: _____

_____
_____
_____

Evening Reflection:

_____
_____
_____
_____

Curiosity is one of the most permanent and certain
characteristics of a vigorous intellect.
—Samuel Johnson

Sight: _____

_____
_____
_____

Smell: _____

_____
_____
_____

Touch: _____

_____
_____
_____

Taste: _____

_____
_____
_____

Hearing: _____

_____
_____
_____

Evening Reflection:

_____
_____
_____
_____

> Even the largest avalanche is triggered by small things.
> —Vernor Vinge

Sight: _____

_____

_____

_____

Smell: _____

_____

_____

_____

Touch: _____

_____

_____

_____

Taste: _____

_____

_____

_____

Hearing: _____

_____

_____

_____

Evening Reflection:

_____

_____

_____

_____

I think, at a child's birth, if a mother could ask a fairy godmother
to endow it with the most useful gift, that gift should be curiosity.
—Eleanor Roosevelt

Sight: _____

_____

_____

_____

Smell: _____

_____

_____

_____

Touch: _____

_____

_____

_____

Taste: _____

_____

_____

_____

Hearing: _____

_____

_____

_____

Evening Reflection:

_____

_____

_____

_____

The true secret of happiness lies in taking a genuine
interest in all the details of daily life.
—William Morris

Sight: _____
_____
_____
_____

Smell: _____
_____
_____
_____

Touch: _____
_____
_____
_____

Taste: _____
_____
_____
_____

Hearing: _____
_____
_____
_____

Evening Reflection:
_____
_____
_____
_____

Recommendation: One day this week, use a stimulus you do not like.

Sight: _____

_____
_____
_____

Smell: _____

_____
_____
_____

Touch: _____

_____
_____
_____

Taste: _____

_____
_____
_____

Hearing: _____

_____
_____
_____

Evening Reflection:

_____
_____
_____
_____

We keep moving forward, opening new doors, and doing new things, because we're curious and curiosity keeps leading us down new paths.
—Walt Disney

Sight: _____

_____

_____

_____

Smell: _____

_____

_____

_____

Touch: _____

_____

_____

_____

Taste: _____

_____

_____

_____

Hearing: _____

_____

_____

_____

Evening Reflection:

_____

_____

_____

_____

From wonder into wonder existence opens.
—Lao Tzu

Sight: _____
_____
_____
_____

Smell: _____
_____
_____
_____

Touch: _____
_____
_____
_____

Taste: _____
_____
_____
_____

Hearing: _____
_____
_____
_____

Evening Reflection:

_____
_____
_____
_____

It's the little details that are vital. Little
things make big things happen.
—John Wooden

Sight: _____

_____
_____
_____

Smell: _____

_____
_____
_____

Touch: _____

_____
_____
_____

Taste: _____

_____
_____
_____

Hearing: _____

_____
_____
_____

Evening Reflection:

_____
_____
_____
_____

Mystery creates wonder and wonder is the
basis of man's desire to understand.
—Neil Armstrong

Sight: _____

_____
_____
_____

Smell: _____

_____
_____
_____

Touch: _____

_____
_____
_____

Taste: _____

_____
_____
_____

Hearing: _____

_____
_____
_____

Evening Reflection:

_____
_____
_____
_____

It is the harmony of the diverse parts, their symmetry, their
happy balance; in a word it is all that introduces order,
all that gives unity, that permits us to see clearly and to
comprehend at once both the ensemble and the details.
—Henri Poincare

Sight: _____

_____
_____
_____

Smell: _____

_____
_____
_____

Touch: _____

_____
_____
_____

Taste: _____

_____
_____
_____

Hearing: _____

_____
_____
_____

Evening Reflection:

_____
_____
_____
_____

The aware mind allows you to enjoy the
inherent aliveness in all things.
—Richard Rohr

Sight: _____

_____

_____

_____

Smell: _____

_____

_____

_____

Touch: _____

_____

_____

_____

Taste: _____

_____

_____

_____

Hearing: _____

_____

_____

_____

Evening Reflection:

_____

_____

_____

_____

Recommendation: Use one stimulus for all the senses for one day.

Sight: _____

_____
_____
_____

Smell: _____

_____
_____
_____

Touch: _____

_____
_____
_____

Taste: _____

_____
_____
_____

Hearing: _____

_____
_____
_____

Evening Reflection:

_____
_____
_____
_____

I learned no detail was too small. It was all about the details.
—Brad Grey

Sight: _____

_____

_____

_____

Smell: _____

_____

_____

_____

Touch: _____

_____

_____

_____

Taste: _____

_____

_____

_____

Hearing: _____

_____

_____

_____

Evening Reflection:

_____

_____

_____

_____

I think of myself as quite a shy person. But when I'm curious
about something, I'll go quite far to satisfy my curiosity.
—Alain de Botton

Sight: _____

_____
_____
_____

Smell: _____

_____
_____
_____

Touch: _____

_____
_____
_____

Taste: _____

_____
_____
_____

Hearing: _____

_____
_____
_____

Evening Reflection:

_____
_____
_____
_____

Stillness as a technique is still really captivating to me.
—Adam Baldwin

Sight: _____

_____
_____
_____

Smell: _____

_____
_____
_____

Touch: _____

_____
_____
_____

Taste: _____

_____
_____
_____

Hearing: _____

_____
_____
_____

Evening Reflection:

_____
_____
_____
_____

When was the last time you spent a quiet moment just doing
nothing—just sitting and looking at the sea, or watching the
wind blowing the tree limbs, or waves rippling on a pond,
a flickering candle or children playing in the park?
—Ralph Marston

Sight: _____

_____

_____

_____

Smell: _____

_____

_____

_____

Touch: _____

_____

_____

_____

Taste: _____

_____

_____

_____

Hearing: _____

_____

_____

_____

Evening Reflection:

_____

_____

_____

_____

The beginning of philosophy is to feel a sense of wonder.
—Plato

Sight: _____

_____

_____

_____

Smell: _____

_____

_____

_____

Touch: _____

_____

_____

_____

Taste: _____

_____

_____

_____

Hearing: _____

_____

_____

_____

Evening Reflection:

_____

_____

_____

_____

Study nature, love nature, stay close to nature. It will never fail you.
—Frank Lloyd Wright

Sight: _____

_____
_____
_____

Smell: _____

_____
_____
_____

Touch: _____

_____
_____
_____

Taste: _____

_____
_____
_____

Hearing: _____

_____
_____
_____

Evening Reflection:

_____
_____
_____
_____

Just living is not enough, one must have
sunshine, freedom, and a little flower.
—Hans Christian Andersen

Sight: _____

_____

_____

_____

Smell: _____

_____

_____

_____

Touch: _____

_____

_____

_____

Taste: _____

_____

_____

_____

Hearing: _____

_____

_____

_____

Evening Reflection:

_____

_____

_____

_____

An understanding of the natural world and what's in it is a
source of not only a great curiosity but great fulfillment.
—David Attenborough

Sight: _____

_____

_____

_____

Smell: _____

_____

_____

_____

Touch: _____

_____

_____

_____

Taste: _____

_____

_____

_____

Hearing: _____

_____

_____

_____

Evening Reflection:

_____

_____

_____

_____

Adopt the pace of nature: her secret is patience.
—Ralph Waldo Emerson

Sight: _____

_____

_____

_____

Smell: _____

_____

_____

_____

Touch: _____

_____

_____

_____

Taste: _____

_____

_____

_____

Hearing: _____

_____

_____

_____

Evening Reflection:

_____

_____

_____

_____

While it may seem small, the ripple effects
of small things is extraordinary.
—Matt Bevin

Sight: _____

_____
_____
_____

Smell: _____

_____
_____
_____

Touch: _____

_____
_____
_____

Taste: _____

_____
_____
_____

Hearing: _____

_____
_____
_____

Evening Reflection:

_____
_____
_____
_____

Congratulations!

You have just finished your first thirty days with the *Five-Senses Journal*. You have been mastering the skill of noticing the world around you and putting your experience into words. Your next step is to take those outside experiences and begin to observe how they affect your inner world. Keep going—you will thank yourself for your perseverance.

PART II

Observe

The second step is to use your senses and eye for detail to turn toward your inner world. Instead of focusing on the stimulus chosen, you will focus and describe your inner state in relation to your experience with the stimulus. The mind and body will associate many stimuli with certain feelings and thoughts.

The identification of the change within you is the next step in the process. You will learn to describe your inner states, the subtle differences in them, and how your mind or body can feel these inner states without even meaning to. For example, you might smell fresh-baked cookies, notice that your thoughts go to your childhood, and feel secure and safe. In another example, you might feel a blanket that is rough, notice feelings of discomfort, and begin to bring up memories of an uncomfortable situation. You might describe a tingle in your nose or your heartbeat increasing.

The inner world is both physical and emotional—consider all aspects of what you are observing. None of these feelings are to be interpreted as good or bad; they simply are. Using your senses, you will learn to observe your inner experience with awareness.

Example

With an eye made quiet by the power of harmony, and
the deep power of joy, we see into the life of things.
—William Wordsworth

Sight: _____ "In the Skerries" by Anders Zorn _____

My eyes moved from top to bottom and then left to right. I started by
focusing on details of the painting and then took in the entire painting
as a whole. I began to feel a sense of adventure and confidence building
in my body as I took in the painting.

Smell: _____ *Joy* by OSHO _____

I notice the scent of the book more in my left nostril and then in my
right. It brings up memories of spending time in my favorite book store.
It creates feelings of nostalgia.

Touch: _____ Pink Tourmaline _____

While holding this gem, I felt the roughness in my hands in comparison
to the smooth finish of the gem. Even though a lot of energy was present
in my body, I felt calm while holding the gem. The energy in my body
seemed to focus around my root chakra.

Taste: _____ Chocolate _____

The bittersweet taste of the chocolate spreads across my tongue, and
there was a sense of calm and relaxation after a few bites. It reminded
me of night, which is when I typically eat dark chocolate.

Hearing: _____"For Real" by Winston Surfshirt_____

An energy went to my chest and then flowed through my body. My body began to sway slightly with the music. I felt excited and energized from the song.

Evening Reflection:

Looking into the internal states was much different than describing the external items. I found it interesting that with each item, there was a different level of internal energy and the location of energy varied. My biggest takeaway was the difference in emotions that was instantly felt by changing the stimulus.

It's no wonder that truth is stranger than
fiction. Fiction has to make sense.
—Mark Twain

Sight: _____

_____
_____
_____

Smell: _____

_____
_____
_____

Touch: _____

_____
_____
_____

Taste: _____

_____
_____
_____

Hearing: _____

_____
_____
_____

Evening Reflection:

_____
_____
_____
_____

The details are not the details. They make the design.
—Charles Eames

Sight: _____

_____

_____

_____

Smell: _____

_____

_____

_____

Touch: _____

_____

_____

_____

Taste: _____

_____

_____

_____

Hearing: _____

_____

_____

_____

Evening Reflection:

_____

_____

_____

_____

Recommendation: One day this week, use a stimulus you do not like.

Sight: _____

_____

_____

_____

Smell: _____

_____

_____

_____

Touch: _____

_____

_____

_____

Taste: _____

_____

_____

_____

Hearing: _____

_____

_____

_____

Evening Reflection:

_____

_____

_____

_____

The other is not the source; the source is always within you.
—OSHO

Sight: _____

_____

_____

_____

Smell: _____

_____

_____

_____

Touch: _____

_____

_____

_____

Taste: _____

_____

_____

_____

Hearing: _____

_____

_____

_____

Evening Reflection:

_____

_____

_____

_____

How can one understand that part of you
which does the understanding?
—Upanishads II: 4, 14

Sight: _____

_____

_____

_____

Smell: _____

_____

_____

_____

Touch: _____

_____

_____

_____

Taste: _____

_____

_____

_____

Hearing: _____

_____

_____

_____

Evening Reflection:

_____

_____

_____

_____

The older I get, the more I'm conscious of ways very small
things can make a change in the world. Tiny little things,
but the world is made up of tiny matters, isn't it?
—Sandra Cisneros

Sight: _____

_____
_____
_____

Smell: _____

_____
_____
_____

Touch: _____

_____
_____
_____

Taste: _____

_____
_____
_____

Hearing: _____

_____
_____
_____

Evening Reflection:

_____
_____
_____
_____

Childhood, after all, is not an ending, but
rather a state full of potent curiosity.
—Rachel Cusk

Sight: _____

_____
_____
_____

Smell: _____

_____
_____
_____

Touch: _____

_____
_____
_____

Taste: _____

_____
_____
_____

Hearing: _____

_____
_____
_____

Evening Reflection:

_____
_____
_____
_____

One sees great things from the valley; only
small things from the peak.
—Gilbert K. Chesterton

Sight: _____

_____
_____
_____

Smell: _____

_____
_____
_____

Touch: _____

_____
_____
_____

Taste: _____

_____
_____
_____

Hearing: _____

_____
_____
_____

Evening Reflection:

_____
_____
_____
_____

To know yourself as the Being underneath the thinker,
the stillness underneath the mental noise, the love and joy
underneath the pain, is freedom, salvation, enlightenment.
—Eckhart Tolle

Sight: _____

_____

_____

_____

Smell: _____

_____

_____

_____

Touch: _____

_____

_____

_____

Taste: _____

_____

_____

_____

Hearing: _____

_____

_____

_____

Evening Reflection:

_____

_____

_____

_____

Recommendation: Use one stimulus for all the senses for one day.

Sight: _____

_____

_____

_____

Smell: _____

_____

_____

_____

Touch: _____

_____

_____

_____

Taste: _____

_____

_____

_____

Hearing: _____

_____

_____

_____

Evening Reflection:

_____

_____

_____

_____

Only I can change my life. No one can do it for me.
—Carol Burnett

Sight: _____

_____
_____
_____

Smell: _____

_____
_____
_____

Touch: _____

_____
_____
_____

Taste: _____

_____
_____
_____

Hearing: _____

_____
_____
_____

Evening Reflection:

_____
_____
_____
_____

Life is 10 percent what happens to you and
90 percent how you react to it.
—Charles R. Swindoll

Sight: _____

_____
_____
_____

Smell: _____

_____
_____
_____

Touch: _____

_____
_____
_____

Taste: _____

_____
_____
_____

Hearing: _____

_____
_____
_____

Evening Reflection:

_____
_____
_____
_____

Live as if you were to die tomorrow. Learn
as if you were to live forever.
—Mahatma Gandhi

Sight: _____

_____
_____
_____

Smell: _____

_____
_____
_____

Touch: _____

_____
_____
_____

Taste: _____

_____
_____
_____

Hearing: _____

_____
_____
_____

Evening Reflection:

_____
_____
_____
_____

Never lose an opportunity of seeing anything
beautiful, for beauty is God's handwriting.
—Ralph Waldo Emerson

Sight: _____
_____
_____
_____

Smell: _____
_____
_____
_____

Touch: _____
_____
_____
_____

Taste: _____
_____
_____
_____

Hearing: _____
_____
_____
_____

Evening Reflection:
_____
_____
_____
_____

Patience is not simply the ability to wait—it's
how we behave while we're waiting.
—Joyce Meyer

Sight: _____

_____

_____

_____

Smell: _____

_____

_____

_____

Touch: _____

_____

_____

_____

Taste: _____

_____

_____

_____

Hearing: _____

_____

_____

_____

Evening Reflection:

_____

_____

_____

_____

I know that I am intelligent, because I know that I know nothing.
—Socrates

Sight: _____

_____
_____
_____

Smell: _____

_____
_____
_____

Touch: _____

_____
_____
_____

Taste: _____

_____
_____
_____

Hearing: _____

_____
_____
_____

Evening Reflection:

_____
_____
_____
_____

Recommendation: Use a person once this week during your practice. For example, you can hold someone's hand, feel their skin against yours, look deeply into their eyes, or taste their lips.

Sight: _____

_____

_____

_____

Smell: _____

_____

_____

_____

Touch: _____

_____

_____

_____

Taste: _____

_____

_____

_____

Hearing: _____

_____

_____

_____

Evening Reflection:

_____

_____

_____

_____

Everything that's created comes out of silence. Your thoughts emerge from the nothingness of silence. Your words come out of this void. Your very essence emerged from emptiness. All creativity requires some stillness.
—Wayne Dyer

Sight: _____

_____

_____

_____

Smell: _____

_____

_____

_____

Touch: _____

_____

_____

_____

Taste: _____

_____

_____

_____

Hearing: _____

_____

_____

_____

Evening Reflection:

_____

_____

_____

_____

Cowards die many times before their deaths; the
valiant never taste of death but once.
—William Shakespeare

Sight: _____

_____
_____
_____

Smell: _____

_____
_____
_____

Touch: _____

_____
_____
_____

Taste: _____

_____
_____
_____

Hearing: _____

_____
_____
_____

Evening Reflection:

_____
_____
_____
_____

Mixed feelings, like mixed drinks, are a confusion to the soul.
—George Carman

Sight: _____

_____
_____
_____

Smell: _____

_____
_____
_____

Touch: _____

_____
_____
_____

Taste: _____

_____
_____
_____

Hearing: _____

_____
_____
_____

Evening Reflection:

_____
_____
_____
_____

Follow effective action with quiet reflection. From the
quiet reflection will come even more effective action.
—Peter Drucker

Sight: _____

_____
_____
_____

Smell: _____

_____
_____
_____

Touch: _____

_____
_____
_____

Taste: _____

_____
_____
_____

Hearing: _____

_____
_____
_____

Evening Reflection:

_____
_____
_____
_____

There are no rules of architecture for a castle in the clouds.
—Gilbert K. Chesterton

Sight: _____

_____

_____

_____

Smell: _____

_____

_____

_____

Touch: _____

_____

_____

_____

Taste: _____

_____

_____

_____

Hearing: _____

_____

_____

_____

Evening Reflection:

_____

_____

_____

_____

Replace judgment with curiosity.
—Lynn Nottage

Sight: _____

_____
_____
_____

Smell: _____

_____
_____
_____

Touch: _____

_____
_____
_____

Taste: _____

_____
_____
_____

Hearing: _____

_____
_____
_____

Evening Reflection:

_____
_____
_____
_____

With an eye made quiet by the power of harmony, and
the deep power of joy, we see into the life of things.
—William Wordsworth

Sight: _____

_____

_____

_____

Smell: _____

_____

_____

_____

Touch: _____

_____

_____

_____

Taste: _____

_____

_____

_____

Hearing: _____

_____

_____

_____

Evening Reflection:

_____

_____

_____

_____

Honesty is the first chapter in the book of wisdom.
—Thomas Jefferson

Sight: _____

_____
_____
_____

Smell: _____

_____
_____
_____

Touch: _____

_____
_____
_____

Taste: _____

_____
_____
_____

Hearing: _____

_____
_____
_____

Evening Reflection:

_____
_____
_____
_____

Thoughts are the shadows of our feelings—
always darker, emptier, and simpler.
—Friedrich Nietzsche

Sight: _____

_____

_____

_____

Smell: _____

_____

_____

_____

Touch: _____

_____

_____

_____

Taste: _____

_____

_____

_____

Hearing: _____

_____

_____

_____

Evening Reflection:

_____

_____

_____

_____

Curiosity will conquer fear even more than bravery will.
—James Stephens

Sight: _____

_____

_____

_____

Smell: _____

_____

_____

_____

Touch: _____

_____

_____

_____

Taste: _____

_____

_____

_____

Hearing: _____

_____

_____

_____

Evening Reflection:

_____

_____

_____

_____

Some people walk in the rain—others just get wet.
—Roger Miller

Sight: _____

_____

_____

_____

Smell: _____

_____

_____

_____

Touch: _____

_____

_____

_____

Taste: _____

_____

_____

_____

Hearing: _____

_____

_____

_____

Evening Reflection:

_____

_____

_____

_____

Every great dream begins with a dreamer. Always remember,
you have within you the strength, the patience, and the
passion to reach for the stars to change the world.
—Harriet Tubman

Sight: _____

_____
_____
_____

Smell: _____

_____
_____
_____

Touch: _____

_____
_____
_____

Taste: _____

_____
_____
_____

Hearing: _____

_____
_____
_____

Evening Reflection:

_____
_____
_____
_____

Develop a passion for learning. If you do,
you will never cease to grow.
—Anthony J. D'Angelo

Sight: _____

_____
_____
_____

Smell: _____

_____
_____
_____

Touch: _____

_____
_____
_____

Taste: _____

_____
_____
_____

Hearing: _____

_____
_____
_____

Evening Reflection:

_____
_____
_____
_____

Congratulations!

You have finished sixty days in your *Five-Senses Journal*. You now know how to fully notice the details in your environment, and you can turn your focus to your inner world to assess what is happening within you. The ability to analyze your inner states and experiences is yours.

The next step is to begin to drop the words and labels and be with those states. It gets a bit esoteric here, but the idea is to drop the labels and fully experience the states within you. This is known as stillness, and it will be the final thirty days in your journey.

PART III

Stillness

The final step in the progression is stillness. This is also known as *nonjudgmental observation*. In this sense, judgment is not good or bad, right or wrong. For this work, the word *judgment* is closer to the definition of the word *label*. Through your senses, you take in the stimulus for what it is and see how that connects with your inner world.

Use all your senses now to begin the process. You start with the external to find a connection with the stimulus, and then you move the experience inward as you observe your inner state. From this point, we want to drop those words, memories, notions, and thoughts so we can feel without labels.

Stillness is not based on labels, words, emotions, or feelings. The connection is based in letting go and silence. For example, you may begin to notice a book on the end table. You feel the pages, smell the Musty scent, and see the title. It begins to create an inner experience, and you observe a sense of calm and inquiry. These currently are labeled in your mind. Then you drop the labels and just experience— the thoughts no longer persist. All judgments, ideas, or preconceived notions are dropped. You simply are in the moment, a moment created by the initial experience of the book.

For this part, there is an open journaling section where you can express your experience on paper (or not) however you so choose. Perhaps words are not the best way to describe your experience: draw a picture, hum a melody, write a poem, or do a dance. It is your experience— represent it any way you like.

Example

Recommendation: Use a person once this week during your practice. For example: you can hold someone's hand and feel their skin against yours, look deeply into their eyes, or taste their lips.

Rose-My Love

The gateway to your soul draws me in

Wrapping me in it's warm embrace, it pulls on me

My heart, spirit, and soul enter into your infinite space

Leaving me without senses or understanding

Deeper and deeper I fall, energies colliding

This place is beyond reality, yet more familiar than my own skin

I am enveloped in your light and darkness

Hold me here, allow me to bask in your divinity

It is here I find myself, it is here I find ...

LOVE

Evening Reflection:

Today I did the weekly recommendation and did soul or eye gazing. We looked into each other's eyes for five minutes without talking. There was a difference in looking into the right eye compared to the left. There was an emotional response while looking into the left eye ... I would like to explore this more.

God is in the details.
—Ludwig Mies van der Rohe

Evening Reflection:

Love is three-quarters curiosity.
—Giacomo Casanova

Evening Reflection:

Recommendation: Use a person once this week during your practice. For example, you can hold someone's hand and feel their skin against yours, look deeply into their eyes, or taste their lips.

Evening Reflection:

In the midst of movement and chaos, keep stillness inside of you.
—Deepak Chopra

Evening Reflection:

Love is misunderstood to be an emotion; actually,
it is a state of awareness, a way of being in the
world, a way of seeing oneself and others.
—David R. Hawkins

Evening Reflection:

It may be that our cosmic curiosity ... is a genetically encoded
force that we illuminate when we look up and wonder.
—Neil deGrasse Tyson

Evening Reflection:

Curiosity is the one thing invincible in Nature.
—Freya Stark

Evening Reflection:

So the darkness shall be the light, and the stillness the dancing.
—T. S. Eliot

Evening Reflection:

Eternity is not simply outside the moment of time
but at the heart of each moment, and this eternity,
present within time, gives to time its true value.
—Bishop Kallistos Ware

Evening Reflection:

The best remedy for those who are afraid, lonely, or unhappy is to go outside, somewhere where they can be quiet, alone with the heavens, nature, and God. Because only then does one feel that all is as it should be.
—Anne Frank

Evening Reflection:

The best cure for the body is a quiet mind.
—Napoleon Bonaparte

Evening Reflection:

Recommendation: One day this week, use a stimulus you do not like.

Evening Reflection:

It all comes down to being present. Everyone in your life is craving, more than anything, for you to show up with all of you in your body and be present. That is what really gives nourishment.
—John Gray

Evening Reflection:

Harmony makes small things grow—lack
of it makes great things decay.
—Sallust

Evening Reflection:

For life and death are one, even as the river and the sea are one.
—Khalil Gibran

Evening Reflection:

Every flower is a soul blossoming in nature.
—Gérard De Nerval

Evening Reflection:

There is a wisdom of the head and a wisdom of the heart.
—Charles Dickens

Evening Reflection:

God gave us the gift of life; it is up to us to
give ourselves the gift of living well.
—Voltaire

Evening Reflection:

A beautiful woman delights the eye; a wise woman,
the understanding; a pure one, the soul.
—Minna Antrim.

Evening Reflection:

The ego is nothing other than the focus of conscious attention.
—Alan Watts

Evening Reflection:

Your talent is God's gift to you. What you
do with it is your gift back to God.
—Leo Buscaglia

Evening Reflection:

When you love someone, the best thing you can offer is
your presence. How can you love if you are not there?
—Thich Nhat Hanh

Evening Reflection:

Recommendation: Find stillness with an item for at least ten minutes.

Evening Reflection:

If you don't love me, it does not matter,
anyway I can love for both of us.
—Stendhal

Evening Reflection:

He is happiest, be he king or peasant, who finds peace in his home.
—Johann Wolfgang von Goethe

Evening Reflection:

You can't depend on your eyes when your imagination is out of focus.
—Mark Twain

Evening Reflection:

The purpose of art is washing the dust of daily life off our souls.
—Pablo Picasso

Evening Reflection:

Love is the silent saying and saying of a single name.
—Mignon McLaughlin

Evening Reflection:

While I thought that I was learning how to
live, I have been learning how to die.
—Leonardo da Vinci

Evening Reflection:

Learning how to be still, to really be still and let life happen—
that stillness becomes a radiance. —Morgan Freeman

Evening Reflection:

Congratulations!

You completed all ninety days in the *Five-Senses Journal.* You now have access to the minute details in any object or moment. You have the power to go inside and know how you are feeling and what you are experiencing. Then, whenever you choose, you can go further, dropping it all, and find that silence and stillness.

At any point, you can call upon this power and be fully present to whichever degree you so choose. Take some time and sit back. Allow the feeling of completing this to wash over you and enjoy it. Even though your ninety days are over, continue to do the exercises. This is a skill that must be used to be maintained.

Thank you for taking the time to work on this for yourself. Change in the world starts with you—now go out and make the change you want to see.

Appendix A

Sound Words

hanging	croaking	laughing	ringing	tinkling	barking,	crunching,	moaning	rumbling
thudding	bawling	crying	mooing	rustling	thumping	blaring	dripping	mumbling
scratching	ticking	booming	exploding	muttering	screaming	twittering	buzzing	fizzing
noisy	screeching	warbling	chattering	gagging	peeping	singing	wheezing	chiming
gasping	piercing	slamming	whimpering	chirping	giggling	pinging	shouting	whining
clanging	grating	plopping	silent	whispering	clicking	grunting	quacking	snoring
whooping	clinking	gurgling	quiet	splashing	cooing	hissing	rapping	squawking
coughing	honking	rasping	stuttering	crackling	jangling	riming	tearing	creaking

Touch Words

abrasive	feathery	knobbed	sandy	spongy	biting	fine	lacy	scalding
steamy	boiling	fluffy	leathery	scorching	steely	bubby	foamy	light
scratchy	sticky	bulky	freezing	lukewarm	scummy	stifled	bumpy	furry
matted	shaggy	stinging	burning	fuzzy	metallic	sharp	stony	bushy
glassy	moist	silky	stubby	clammy	gluey	mushy	slimy	tangled
coarse	grainy	numbing	slippery	tender	cool	greasy	oily	sloppy
tepid	cottony	gritty	piercing	smooth	thick	crisp	gushy	plastic
smothering	tickling	touch	words	cushioned	hairy	pocked	soapy	tough
damp	heavy	pointed	soft	velvety	downy	hot	pulpy	sopping
warm	drenched	humid	rocky	soupy	waxy	fragile	sturdy	smooth

Taste and Smell Words

dank	acid	doughy	minty	rank	sweaty	acidic	earthy	moist
raw	sweet	acrid	floury	moldy	rich	tangy	alkaline	flowery
musky	rotten	tasteless	aromatic	fresh	musty	salty	tough	biting
fruity	oily	scented	vile	bitter	garlicky	perfumed	sharp	vinegary
bland	hearty	pickled	sour	burnt	hot	piney	spicy	buttery
lemony	plastic	spoiled	cold	medicinal	pungent	stagnant	woody	fresh

Sight Words

abrasive	feathery	knobbed	sandy	spongy	biting	fine	lacy	scalding
steamy	boiling	fluffy	leathery	scorching	steely	bubbly	foamy	light
scratchy	sticky	bulky	freezing	lukewarm	scummy	stifled	bumpy	furry
matted	shaggy	stinging	burning	fuzzy	metallic	sharp	stony	bushy
glassy	moist	silky	stubby	clammy	gluey	mushy	slimy	tangled
coarse	grainy	numbing	slippery	tender	cool	greasy	oily	sloppy
tepid	cottony	gritty	piercing	smooth	thick	crisp	gushy	plastic
smothering	tickling	cushioned	hairy	pocked	soapy	tough	damp	heavy
pointed	soft	velvety	downy	hot	pulpy	sopping	warm	drenched
humid	rocky	soupy	waxy	balanced	glittery	matte	swift	meandering

List of sensory words from http://www.waunakee.k12.wi.us/faculty/lcarothers/EffectiveWriting/Descriptive/Sensory%20Words.pdf

Feelings List

Affectionate

compassionate
friendly
loving
open hearted
sympathetic
tender
warm

Engaged

absorbed
alert
curious
engrossed
enchanted
entranced
fascinated
interested
intrigued
involved

spellbound
stimulated

Hopeful

expectant
encouraged
optimistic

Confident

empowered
open
proud
safe
secure

Excited

amazed
animated
ardent

aroused
astonished
dazzled
eager
energetic
enthusiastic
giddy
invigorated
lively
passionate
surprised
vibrant

Grateful

appreciative
moved
thankful
touched

Inspired

amazed
awed
wonder

Joyful

amused
delighted
glad
happy
jubilant
pleased
tickled

Exhilarated

blissful
ecstatic
elated
enthralled
exuberant
radiant
rapturous
thrilled

Peaceful

calm
clear headed
comfortable
centered
content

Equanimeous

fulfilled
mellow
quiet
relaxed
relieved
satisfied
serene
still
tranquil
trusting

Refreshed

enlivened
rejuvenated
renewed
rested
restored
revived

Afraid

apprehensive
dread
foreboding
frightened
mistrustful
panicked
petrified
scared

suspicious
terrified
wary
worried

Annoyed

aggravated
dismayed
disgruntled
displeased
exasperated
frustrated
impatient
irritated
irked

Angry

enraged
furious
incensed
indignant
irate
livid
outraged
resentful

Aversion

animosity
appalled

contempt
disgusted
dislike
hate
horrified
hostile
repulsed

Confused

ambivalent
baffled
bewildered
dazed
hesitant
lost
mystified
perplexed
puzzled
torn

Disconnected

alienated
aloof
apathetic
bored
cold
detached
distant
distracted
indifferent

numb
removed
uninterested
withdrawn

Disquieted

agitated
alarmed
discombobulated
disconcerted
disturbed
perturbed
rattled
restless
shocked
startled
surprised
troubled
turbulent
turmoil
uncomfortable
uneasy
unnerved
unsettled
upset

Embarrassed

ashamed
chagrined
flustered

guilty
mortified
self-conscious

Fatigued

beat
burnt out
depleted
exhausted
lethargic
listless
sleepy
tired
weary
worn out

Pain

agony
anguished
bereaved
devastated
grief
heartbroken
hurt
lonely
miserable
regretful
remorseful

Sad

depressed
dejected
despair
despondent
disappointed
discouraged
disheartened
forlorn
gloomy
heavy hearted
hopeless
melancholy
unhappy
wretched

Tense

anxious
cranky
distressed
distraught
edgy
fidgety
frazzled
irritable
jittery
nervous
overwhelmed
restless
stressed out

Vulnerable

fragile
guarded
helpless
insecure
leery
reserved
sensitive
shaky

Yearning

envious
jealous
longing
nostalgic
pining

List of feeling words from: https://www.cnvc.org/sites/default/files/feelings_inventory_0.pdf

Appendix C

Root Chakra: Represents our foundation and feeling of being grounded.
> Location: Base of spine in tailbone area.
> Emotional issues: Survival issues like financial independence, money, and food.

Sacral Chakra: Our connection and ability to accept others and new experiences.
> Location: Lower abdomen, two inches below the navel and two inches in.
> Emotional issues: Sense of abundance, well-being, pleasure, and sexuality.

Solar Plexus Chakra: Our ability to be confident and in control of our lives
> Location: Upper abdomen in the stomach area.
> Emotional issues: Self-worth, self-confidence, and self-esteem.

Heart Chakra: Our ability to love.
> Location: Center of chest, just above the heart.
> Emotional issues: Love, joy, and inner peace.

Throat Chakra: Our ability to communicate.
> Location: Throat
> Emotional issues: Communication, self-expression of feelings, and truth.

Third Eye Chakra: Our ability to focus on and see the big picture.
>
> Location: Forehead between the eyes.
>
> Emotional issues: Intuition, imagination, wisdom, and the ability to think and make decisions.

Crown Chakra: The highest chakra represents our ability to be fully connected spiritually.
>
> Location: The very top of the head.
>
> Emotional issues: Inner and outer beauty, our connection to spirituality, and pure bliss.

Chakra list and explanation from: https://www.mindbodygreen.com/0-91/The-7-Chakras-for-Beginners.html

Made in the USA
Monee, IL
18 February 2021

60787914R00076